Variations on
IMMORTAL, INVISIBLE, GOD ONLY WISE

HANS UWE HIELSCHER
Based on the Traditional Welsh Hymn
ST. DENIO

INTRODUCTION

Maestoso

Gt./Sw./Ch.: Foundations (16') 8' 4' 2' Mixt., Man. couplers Gt.
Ped.: Foundations 16' 8' 4', Ped. couplers

F0650
© Copyright 2002 by H. T. FitzSimons Company. All rights reserved. Made in U.S.A.

HYMN

Ch: Solo reed 8′

Sw: Bourdon 8′ 4′

Ped: 16′ 8′

VARIATION 1
Andantino

Gt. & Sw:
Diapasons 8′, Sw/Gt

Ped: 16′ 8′ Sw/Ped

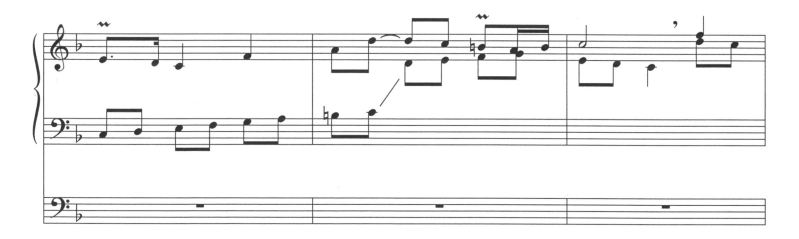

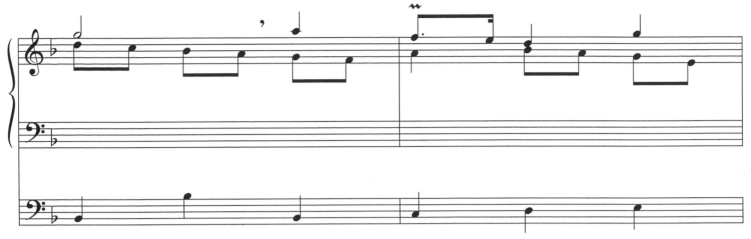

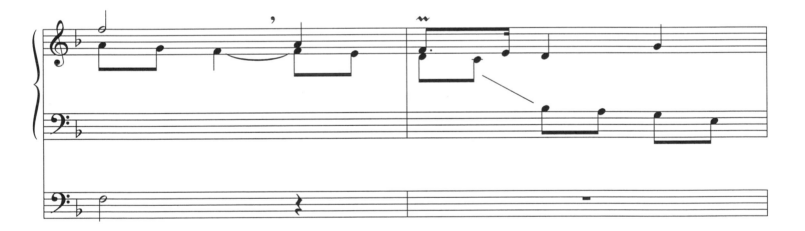

8

VARIATION 2
Allegro

Sw: Cornet 5r

Ch: 8′ 4′

Ped: 16′ 8′

9

10

VARIATION 3
Allegro vivace
Ped: 16´ 8´ 4´ Mixt., reeds

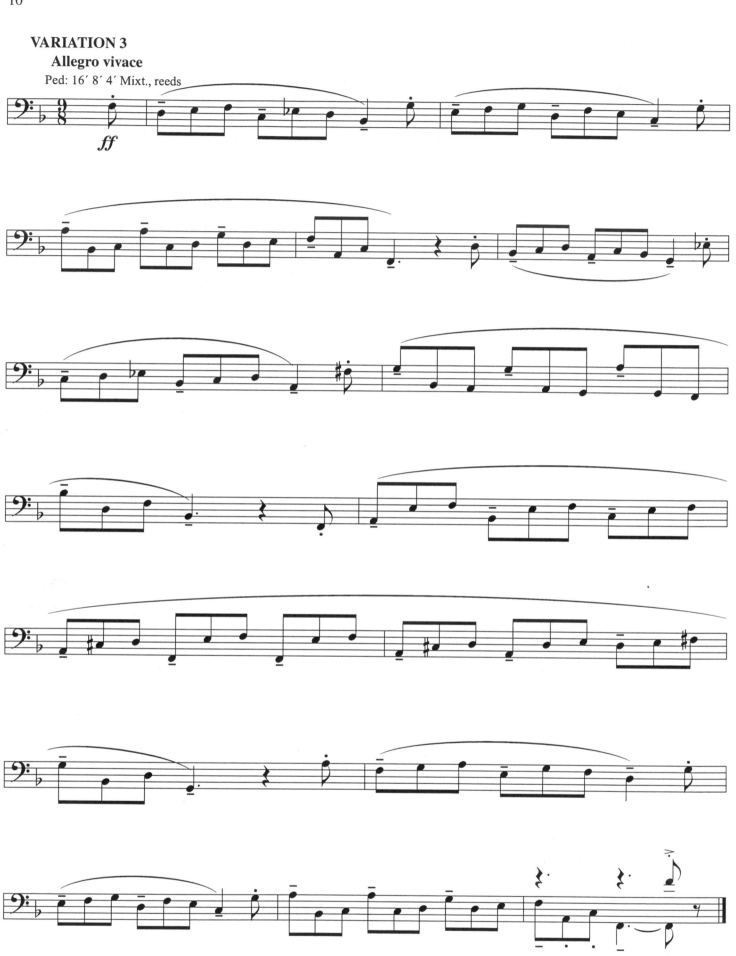

VARIATION 4

Allegro

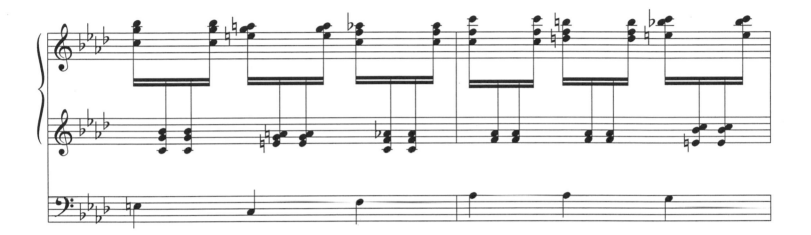

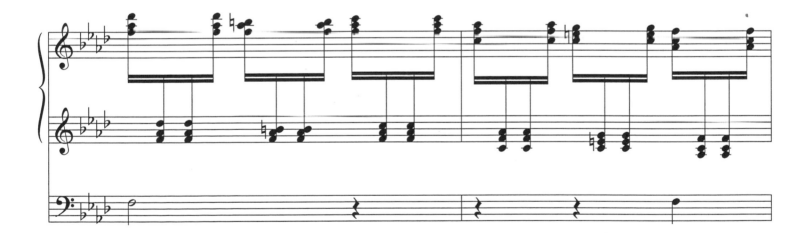

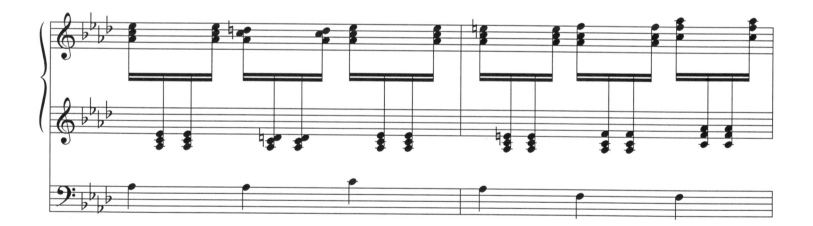

VARIATION 5
Andante

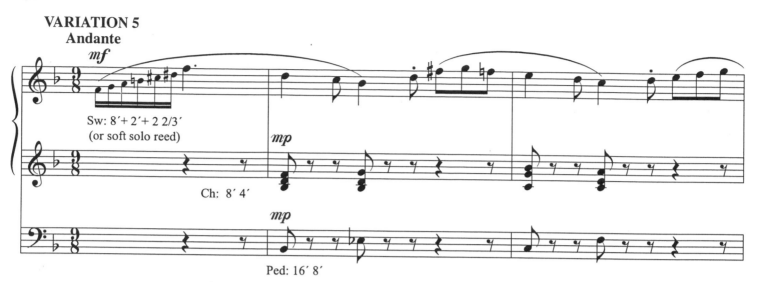

Sw: 8′ + 2′ + 2 2/3′
(or soft solo reed)

Ch: 8′ 4′

Ped: 16′ 8′

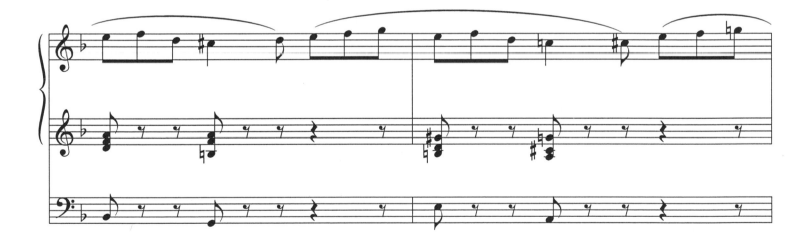

VARIATION 6
Vivace

VARIATION 7

Adagio

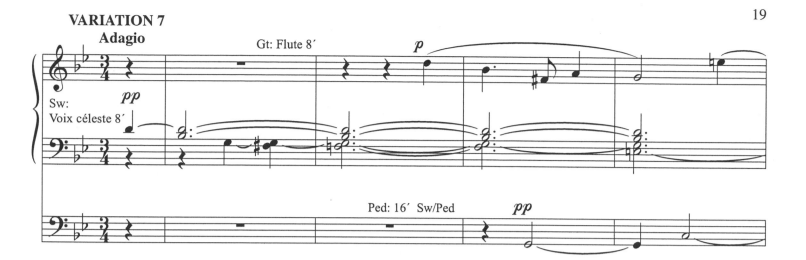

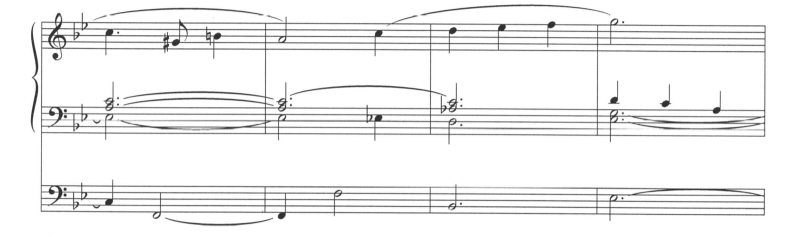

VARIATION 8
Allegretto

sempre non legato

Gt:
Bourdon 8′, Flute 2′

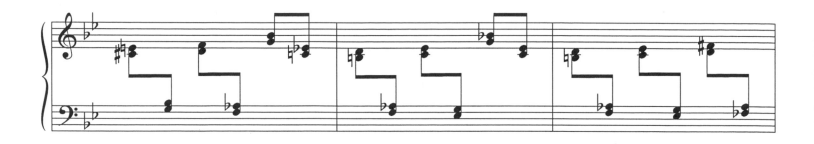

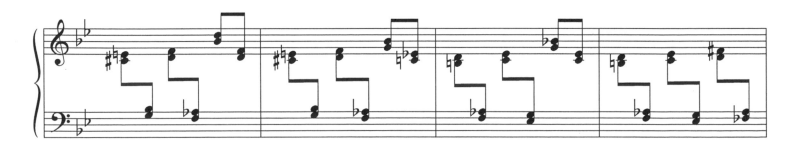

VARIATION 9
Largo

VARIATION 10
Allegro maestoso

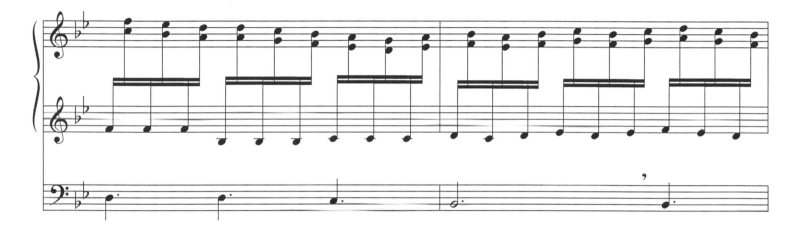

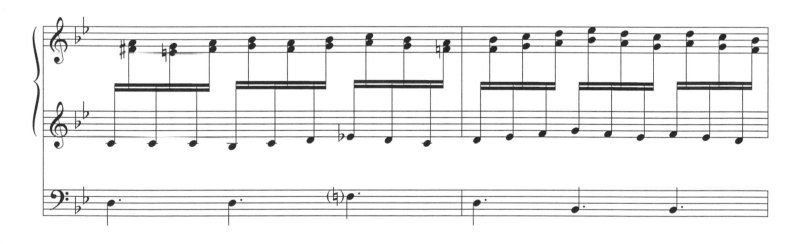

08739792 Variations on

Distributed By
HAL LEONARD

ISBN-13: 978-0-634-08432-4

4.95

ISBN 0-634-08432-1

08739792

9 780634 084324